Great Social Studies Projects™

The Pony Express

Hands-on Projects About Early Communication

Jennifer Quasha

The Rosen Publishing Group's

PowerKids Press™

New York

Some of the projects in this book were designed for a child to do together with an adult.

For Nikki, a great letter writer.

Published in 2001 by The Rosen Publishing Group, Inc.
29 East 21st Street, New York, NY 10010

First Edition

Book Design: Felicity Erwin

Layout: Michael de Guzman

Photo Credits: p. 4 © North Wind Picture Archives; pp. 6 – 21 by Pablo Maldonado.

Quasha, Jennifer.
    The Pony Express: hands-on projects about early communication / by Jennifer Quasha.— 1st ed.
        p. cm.— (Great social studies projects)
    Includes index.
    Summary: Briefly surveys the eighteen-month history of the Pony Express with related projects and activities such as sock
puppets, magnets, and a diorama.
    ISBN 0-8239-5702-0 (alk. paper)
    1. Pony Express—History—Juvenile literature. 2. Postal service—United States—History—Juvenile literature. [1. Pony express. 2. West (U.S.)—History.
3. Handicraft.] I. Title.

HE6375.P65 Q37 2000
383'.143'0973—dc21   00-026676

Manufactured in the United States of America

Contents

The Pony Express

Although the Pony Express only lasted for one and a half years, it forever changed the way that mail was **delivered** in America. Before the Pony Express, mail didn't cross the country very quickly. In the short time that the Pony Express was up and running, Pony Express riders delivered 34,753 pieces of mail and traveled a distance that was equal to more than 20 laps around the earth! The Pony Express came to an end because it cost too much money to run. Still, the Pony Express is one of America's most exciting pieces of history.

Each Pony Express rider would ride at full speed for about 100 miles (161 km) before passing the mail sack to the next rider.

Pony Express Paper-Doll Riders

The advertisement read: "WANTED: Young, skinny, wiry fellows not over the age of 18. Must be **expert** riders willing to risk death daily. **Orphans** preferred. Wages: $25 a week." In 1860, 80 brave men were chosen for the dangerous task of carrying mail from St. Joseph, Missouri, to Sacramento, California, on the Pony Express trail. Each rider rode for awhile, then handed off the mail sack to the next rider.

Here's how to make your own Pony Express rider:

tools and materials

- white cardboard
- scissors
- colored markers
- black construction paper

1 Cut the shape of a man from the white cardboard. Draw and color his skin, face, mustache, and hair.

2 Look at the illustration of the Pony Express riders on page four of this book to get an idea of what riders wore. From the construction paper, cut out items your rider should wear.

3 Leave tabs on the edges of the clothes. The tabs will hold the clothes in place and make it easier to switch the clothes if you choose.

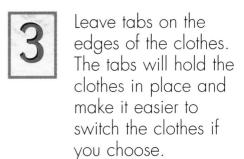

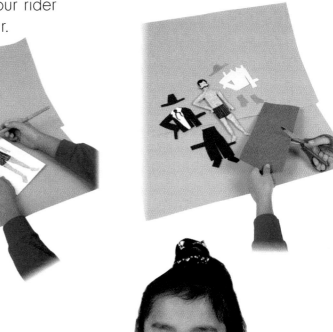

4 You can make different construction-paper outfits for your Pony Express rider to wear.

Pony Express Envelopes

James Jones
156 Beldon Lane
Merriam, Ka 66203

In 1860, letters were the only way that people could **communicate** with each other. There were no telephones, faxes, or even **telegrams**. Writing a letter was the only way to share news. In the mid-1800s, passing news from one American coast to the other took a long time. Lots of letters did not make it all the way across America. Envelopes were used to keep the information in the letters private.

Here's how to make your own envelopes:

tools and materials
- different sizes of white envelopes
- colorful paper (magazine clippings)
- pencil
- glue stick
- white mailing labels

Carefully rip the seams of a regular envelope so that the envelope is completely open.

 Trace the image of the open envelope onto a piece of colorful paper. Then cut out the image of the open envelope from the paper.

 Fold in the flaps of the envelope. Glue side and bottom flaps.

 Place white mailing label on the front of the envelope.

James Jones
156 Beldon Lane
Merriam, Ks 66203

A Pony Sock Puppet

The Pony Express riders rode as fast as possible. The riders had to keep their horses galloping at full speed for as long as they could. The riders would change horses about every 10 to 15 miles (24.1 km) along the way. At these stopping places, the riders switched a tired horse for a well-rested one that could **sprint** the next 15 miles. The Pony Express ponies were young and strong. There were about 500 ponies **available** for the riders to use.

Here's how to make your own pony sock puppet:

tools and materials

- pair of (old) brown socks
- piece of black felt
- scissors
- (15) 10-inch long (25.4-cm-long) pieces of black yarn
- big "googly" eyes
- white glue

Put your hand into one of the socks and decide where you want the horse's face to go.

 Using the felt, cut two triangles for ears and two round nostrils for the nose.

 Glue on a yarn mane, googly eyes, and a felt nose.

 Stuff the other sock inside the front of the horse puppet to give it shape.

A Pony Express Poster

Three men were the **founders** of the Pony Express. Their names were William H. Russell, William B. Waddell, and Alexander Majors. These men ran a successful **freight** business. Their business used **oxen** and wooden wagons to carry goods across America. In order to let people know about their new mail route, the Pony Express founders hung posters in cities and towns. The posters told people how to send a letter using the Pony Express. The posters had pictures and **slogans**.

Here's how to make your own Pony Express poster:

tools and materials

- pencil
- sheet of yellow poster board
- thin and thick colored markers

1 With pencil map out on the poster board the items you would like your Pony Express poster to include. You can use the text and drawings shown or come up with your own ideas.

2 Once you've drawn them in pencil, color in the text and pictures with the markers.

Map of the Pony Express Route

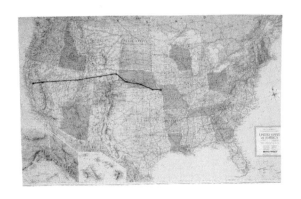

The Pony Express route went from Sacramento, California, to St. Joseph, Missouri, and back again. Riders left a station and headed either east or west depending on their route. At the time, the route went through the Utah, Nebraska, and Kansas territories. Today, those areas are the states of Kansas, Nebraska, Colorado, Wyoming, Utah, and Nevada. The riders went through hundreds of towns and cities.

Here's how to map out your own Pony Express route:

tools and materials

- two pieces of white poster board
- masking tape
- wall map of the United States
- push pins
- two yards (1.8 m) of yarn
- eraser
- scissors

Using masking tape, tape the two pieces of poster board together side by side.

 Center the map over the poster board and fold over the map's edges. Tape the edges down to the back of the board.

 Carefully stick in pins at different locations to show where the Pony Express riders stopped along their route.

 4 Connect the pins with yarn: wrap a section of yarn once around each pin, then move to the next pin. Cut small pieces of eraser to put on backs of pins.

Pony Express Letter-Sack Magnets

The Pony Express riders carried a letter sack filled with about 20 pounds (9 kgs) of mail. They could not carry much more than that because they did not want to put too much weight on top of the horse. A horse could only carry about 165 pounds (75 kgs). The Pony Express riders weighed about 125 pounds (57 kgs) each. Each rider also needed **gear**. Here's how to make your own Pony Express letter-sack magnets:

tools and materials

- brown construction paper
- scissors
- white paper
- black yarn
- thin-tipped black, red, and blue markers
- white glue
- package of round refrigerator magnets

Cut sack shapes from the brown construction paper. Cut six tiny letter-shaped rectangles from the white paper. Cut a six-inch (15-cm) piece of yarn.

 With the markers, sketch mailing labels and stamps onto the letter-shaped rectangles (envelopes).

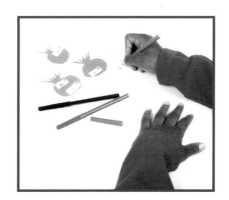

 Glue the envelopes onto the sacks.

 Tie the yarn around the necks of the sacks and glue each sack onto a magnet.

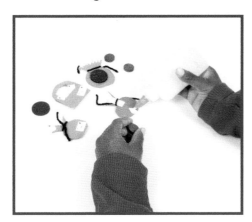

A Pony Express Diorama

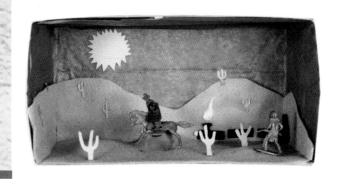

On every ride, the Pony Express riders had to face many **challenges**. There were different weather **conditions** along the route. Sometimes riders needed to get across mountains covered with snow. Other times they had to travel across hot, sandy desert. Riders also came across Native Americans who were not happy to have the riders on their land. Fights often broke out between Native Americans and Pony Express riders.
Here's how to make your own Pony Express **diorama**:

tools and materials

- rectangular box (or shoe box)
- blue tissue paper
- light brown felt (sand-colored)
- white glue
- black, green, and yellow paper
- scissors
- cotton ball
- cowboy, Native American figurines

1 Using the white glue, stick the blue tissue paper and light brown felt to the inside of the shoe box. This will make the sky and sandy plains of the West.

2 From the black construction paper, cut out the shapes of a steam train. From the green construction paper, cut out many cactus plants in all shapes and sizes.

3 Now glue to the diorama the pieces you have cut: the cactus plants and the train. Glue a pinch of the cotton ball "steam" coming from the train.

4 Finally add the Pony Express rider (or cowboy) and Native American figurines.

Pony Express Station-House

There were about 120 stations along the Pony Express route where riders could change horses. These stations were **tended** by about 400 men who cared for the horses that were **stabled** there. At some stations along the way, excited crowds would cheer for riders who arrived. Some stations were near **saloons**. Here's how to make your own Pony Express station-house with a cheering crowd:

tools and materials

- shoe box
- scissors
- white glue
- masking tape
- egg carton
- X-Acto knife

- Popsicle sticks
- yellow construction paper
- black pen
- water-soluble paint
- photos of friends or family
- brown paper

20

Take the lid of a shoe box and cut in half. Cut the long side edges off of one half.

Cover shoe box and the cut lid pieces with brown paper using glue. Stand shoe box on uncut half of lid. Glue cut half of lid to make roof overhang. Tape the two long side edges together. Cut out two yellow squares. Cut out small yellow shape. Write "Saloon" with black pen.

3 Glue yellow squares to shoe box sides for doors. Using only the bottom of egg carton, divide each egg cup and glue together. Using X-Acto knife, slice small slits for Popsicle stick arms and neck. Break Popsicle stick in half. Put half-sticks into arm and neck holes.

4 Paint the egg carton people and glue on photos for their heads.

How to Use Your Projects

You can use your Pony Express projects for school or at home. Decorate your room with the station-house diorama. Entertain your younger sister or brother with the pony sock puppet. Maybe you can bring your Pony Express map to school to use in a school project.

Great social studies projects can make great gifts, too! Perhaps your teacher or parents would like some letter-sack magnets. Remember that the Pony Express was an exciting piece of history. Making and using your Pony Express projects can be exciting, too!

Glossary

available (uh-VAY-luh-bul) Able to be used.

challenges (CHAH-lenj-ez) Things that take effort to complete.

communicate (kuh-MYOO-nih-kayt) To share information or feelings.

conditions (kun-DIH-shunz) A set of acts or events.

delivered (dih-LIH-verd) To have brought something to someone.

diorama (dy-uh-RAM-uh) A small version of a scene that is viewed through an opening.

expert (EK-spert) A person who knows a lot about a subject.

founders (FOWN-durz) The people who start up something, like a town or club.

freight (FRAYT) The goods that a train, boat, or airplane carries.

galloping (GAH-lup-ing) The fastest type of running a horse does.

gear (GEER) Clothes or tools needed for some purpose.

orphans (OR-funz) A child or animal who no longer has parents.

oxen (AKS-in) More than one ox.

saloons (suh-LOON) Bar or tavern.

slogans (SLO-ginz) Words or phrases used by a group to announce its purpose.

sprint (SPRINT) To run at top speed for a short distance.

stabled (STAY-buld) To put or keep an animal in a stable, or shelter.

telegrams (TEL-uh-gramz) Messages sent by telegraph.

tended (TEND-id) Taken care of, looked after.

Index

Web Sites

To learn more about the Pony Express, check out this Web site:

http://www.wco.com/~xptom/